ABOUT THE AUTHOR

Ty'rone (ti-rone) Haughton is a Jamaican born poet from Leicester, a public speaker and advocate for looked after children. Ty'rone's poetry is a vulnerable exploration of society and identity, which has seen him perform internationally and supporting fellow British poets, Akala and John Berkavitch. When he is not facilitating poetry workshops, he is singing nursery rhymes with his children and watering plants. Ty'rone's writing is distinct, it is gentle yet brutal in approach. Ty'rone uses meticulous lyricism and storytelling to invite his audience in before punching them in the throat.

https://www.thaughtonpoetry.com/

Ty'rone Haughton
HOODS

VERVE
POETRY PRESS

BIRMINGHAM

PUBLISHED BY VERVE POETRY PRESS
https://vervepoetrypress.com
mail@vervepoetrypress.com

FIRST PUBLISHED NOV 2022

Printed and bound in the UK
by ImprintDigital, Exeter

ISBN: 978-1-913917-22-7

For Pup, Bounce & Ode

CONTENTS

HOODS

CHILD

July 24th 1997

Gentle Jesus

Gentle Jesus
meek and mild.
Please relieve this
weakened child.
If pepper shall burn
please make his mild
please don't let the world
take his smile.

May his spirit not be bruised
from this physical abuse.
May he stand tall
and not use history as an excuse
but somewhat of a tool
to beat down Babylon
and build up a battalion.
May his words be heard and travel
to all corners of the earth.
I know his birth
was something of worth.

May his pain strengthen others
may he be an example to his brothers.
Guide him
stay beside him
Oh Lord, he is alone.
He must learn to live inside his mind
build worlds from imagination
to create what he sees outside.
I pray this is a process of toughening
this child's life will be very long-suffering.

I pray he knows I will never stop loving him
I know my prayers will cuddle him
I send angels to watch over him.

Lord direct his dreams
for every moment he sleeps.
Manifest every vision he sees
Lord please.
May he always tell the truth
and I pray he never
forgets his roots.

Maroon

Before my soul would know my face
it would roll through time and space.
Its steps traced under the mountains
of a place I would call home.
My soul would learn the ways of the runaways
how to withstand the hardest terrains
and remain the same shape
returning to the same state
regardless of the weight I bear.

It was there
my soul learned resilience.
Long before my earthborn body
heard the snake's sibilance.
My soul would run drills at noon
and stood still at midnight
harnessing the darkness of the dense interior.
My soul lost any sense of inferior.

My soul is the son of soldiers.
Those with strong shoulders
rebellious and stiff-necked.
So when I found myself shipwrecked
abandoned on a new island.
My ancestors knew I would see more cruelty.
They made sure the hurt wouldn't undo me
it is red dirt that runs through me.
Under the moon they gave me cover
my blood is Maroon in colour.

My soul ran from the whip
it would run from the belt
one day my dislocated soul
will run from myself.
Long after this body has expired
the soul it houses will still be exiled.
Its fire will still yearn
my soul has forever had a flame
to keep my soul running
I must resume its burn.

Those who are marooned never return.

Brandon Simmons

You had everything on my wish list.
More than a toy -
Father Christmas missed this boy.
You had joy
and a smile that I wanted
you were a child
that's all I wanted.
You had a dad to hold your hand
and probably still had sand in your trunks
from holidays in the summer months
you had it better than some of us.
I used to watch you on the bus
as you sat there with your mum
I wanted to feel like you just once.

I bet your parents woke you gently
sat on your bed and told you *breakfast is ready*.
Always fed -
I bet they made sure they kept you healthy.
They probably maintained your hygiene
on Fridays you got ice cream
family films on Saturday nights seemed
like the norm to you.
For I, only a pipe dream.
You didn't know how lonely nights feel
you were loved
I wanted to feel like you just once.

I took your name tag from your book bag.
You felt so safe that -
you didn't even look back.
Thought I'd use it only when I needed to.
Though I never said please to you
I've been meaning to
thank you.
Thank you for calling the police
telling them there's brawling on my street
chaos in the house next door to me.
Thank you for the relationships with bus drivers
whom you never met but know you
on a first name basis
your name is known in so many places.
You made me feel normal and know what safe is.
Thank you
for letting me feel like you just once.

If The Door Knocks

Don't answer it.
Stay away from all windows
don't let them know you're inside.
Hide
evade the light
find the shade if you have to.
If the door knocks
under no circumstance must you open it.
Hope doesn't visit where the hopeless live.

There will never be a saviour on the other side
or a concerned passerby
even if the world heard your cries
they will never pry.
If they see you
hide your hurt and tell them I'm at work.
And you're not at school because you fell or you're not well
cover the swelling
in your retelling;
make sure the bruises and contusions came from
tripping over shoestrings.

We live in a polished postcode
where lawns are lush
interiors are plush
the council tax way too much
for them to think you're living rough.
The mise en scène
is deceiving them to believe,
when the cameras leave

the scene won't stop.
But my world is made of props.

If this door could just knock.
If a rat would squeal
if a snake would grass
if a songbird cried
A Karen could Karen
if a wolf or a whistle could blow.
The whole house would fall
and I could leave this show.

Something To Cry About

I got so used to the abuse
I was numb to it.
I was stripped naked
faced with makeshift weapons
intended to make me learn lessons.
Mop sticks, hoover pipes,
ice water soaked leather belts and
anything to cause a swelling.
Scart leads, net curtain wires,
the closest extension cord.
I could hear the whip cracking sound
but I had learned to hold it down before I
Give you something to cry about.

Battered, bruised, bleeding
never got stitches.
I used to be in my briefs
outside in the night time
freezing until my dinner was finished.
Beat the child out of me.
I was never cheesing in pictures
my face always glum so I shun from it
I was throwing up meals and forced to eat the vomit.
Thoughts of leaving this torture house
but it felt like somebody clipped my heels
whenever I tried to run from it.
Now Picture this -
all my Christmas' consisted of expensive gifts
it had the outside world and my friends
thinking I was the luckiest kid.

It distorted my views and had me believing
this is what love really is -
Leveraging and keeping up appearances.
Remember feeling I couldn't speak about my fearfulness
I was just waiting for someone to ask me about my parenting.

I would always show up late and fall asleep at school
all my classmates thought it was great
they would see me as cool
but I just haven't slept in days,
can't recall the last time that I bathed.
The last time I was played with
or the last time I felt safety.

In the peak of scorching summers
I was the only kid sporting jumpers.
Every time we played sports
they had shorts
and I was wearing joggers.

My skin heals so well luckily
but it's the mental scars that still trouble me
I flinch every time my girl touches me.
When you put hands on a child;
that's an evil decision
had a grown man like me
sleeping in the foetal position.

Internal battles to find my zen and bliss
fourteen calendars on this planet
my mattress still had the stench of piss.
Told I'd need counselling because it might hurt to recollect this
all now I haven't found a shrink
I just drown in this ink

I turned words into my therapist.
Always had a fear of sharing the words you're hearing
I was raised without care and had to drag myself here
had to develop an acquired taste to my tears.
I was scared
when I'd hear a certain name spoken.
Then the curtain started closing in
on all the shame I was frozen in
the chains got popped off
the doors got broken in
I chopped the locks off all the pain I'd been holding in.

I've wanted to soak in my sorrows
but I've always been too afraid to swim
so I just put off until tomorrow.
I had no love to borrow
I walked through the depths of many midnights
and had no one to follow
the journey nearly made me hollow.
Nearly made me empty
nearly made me unkind and nearly made me hateful
nearly made me resentful of
the family and adults around me who watched as it started.
They ignored my scars and bruises
I was never safeguarded
never protected
I grown and reflected
learned I was totally neglected -
their memories became selective.
So when I greet them now
I see their frowns and I feel proud
that I exceeded their perspectives and all expectations;
they can't see how I could be standing tall knowing my situation.

Unfortunately,
I'm the result of a failed system.
What can happen when we dismiss the children
they can grow and live as victims
in front of our eyes and under our supervision.
But we can alter these lives
once we choose to look and listen
choose to no longer normalise abuse
and turn our eyes from the truth,
choose to face our own demons and talk to our own traumas
we'll be in a better position to be raising sons and daughters.

Don't Speak

Don't speak
if you get stopped in the streets by police
looking for another nigger to eat.
Another black soul to feed
to the belly of the beast.

What I'm selling is a disease
what I'm telling, listen please.
Don't be like me
though I'm more nuanced than it seems
I too once had dreams
I too once believed we were kings and queens.
But after all I have seen
please excuse my self esteem.

Life's a cycle
more vicious and harder than karma
so I would rather not father a seed in this farmer's land.
For us, this ground will never harvest plans.

Beats And Bars

I grew up on *Roots.*
I grew up on the harshest truths and Heartless Crew.
No love in the house
it was heartless too.

I grew up on Sidewinder and Pure Garage CDs.
Twice as Nice and D Double E.
I grew up on cash not credit
catalogue fraud and jail visits
court hearings and scale digits.

I grew up on *Get Rich or Die Tryin'*
50 Cent was more mantra than man
if you get knocked down nine times
make sure you still stand.
I took Marshall Mathers on all my travels
I grew up on *Hailie's Song* and I grew up on *Stan.*

I grew up on Bounty, Britney, Toni, Whitney.
Every time I heard *It's not right but it's ok*
it hit me.
I grew up on So Solid
no solace
cold porridge
and a whole knowledge
of beats and bars
for whenever the beats were too hard.

I'd write a verse to the body percussion.
DJ scratches and drum kicks
were matched with lyrics that captured
pain and sadness
dismay and anguish.
My saving grace was
finding a language
my tongue couldn't manage.
I grew up in a dangerous house
with pen and pad I found my way out.

Punching Bag

"Why God, why God do I gotta suffer? Pain in my heart carry burdens full of struggle" - Kendrick Lamar, 'Fear'.

"Oh, you're strong!" they say. They told me I was the strongest, toughest and most resilient child they'd ever known. They never said I was fun, cheeky, creative; which I have always been but they didn't value that in the same way they valued how well I could take a punch. I too became less intrigued with my childlike qualities and found pride in being tough. Though, I never saw myself as tough. I think they just couldn't tell the difference between tough and numb. Like a punching bag; tough or just numb?

I would grow to put myself, physically and emotionally in the line of danger. "You're strong" I would tell myself. I only felt safe with danger and conflict, bored to death and confused whenever there was peace. It was thrilling to put my resilience through the bleep test. I wanted to see how far I could go, how long I could last before collapsing. It was a self harming exercise that got me nowhere.

Resilience, I hate it. To be called that today, offends me. Tyres, brick walls and hiking boots should be resilient. Not me. Not a child. I'm soft - comforted by strokes and being the little spoon. I never wanted to be this tough; experiences contoured my profile and coded my spirit. But my face is not my heart. I am a sensitive soul. I am not the dispassionate beast the world hoped I'd become.

Resilience should be reserved for that which is designed to

combat adverse forces; to withstand expected pressures. I wonder, are all boys like me born to withstand? Are we cursed with combat and adversity? Should we expect the world to unleash its evils onto us? Are we the punching bag?

WAR TO WAGE

I have a war to wage.

A bird song from the slaughter's cage
it's a death threat from the author's page
Enormous.
Raucous.
Rage.
Sage couldn't cleanse.

My anger hails from the deepest waters
with a sulphurous stench
gunpowder is my scent.
This fury is so loud
I walk around with a ballistic sound.
How could I ever steer off course
when I'm clearly statistic bound?

My aura is spiky
closed off and off putting
an absent mind, I'm off putting on unkept greens
trying to fill holes from which I still bleed.
Aiming to feel whole as a fractured being
because this war I have to wage
could put the whole world under siege.

Somehow,
I make it to the coastline of my adolescence.
Feet upon the shore
the tide leaves me breathless.
The water is choppy

no father to copy
no role to model
no example to hold onto
no wise voice to score my voyage.

My toolkit is foolish.
I do wish I was more equipped to do this with
righteous teachings
a self esteem that reaches heights
believing I stood a chance In this little life.
Instead I've been
misinformed and ill advised
that the rage was not given
rather, it was all mine.
I fell in line with the doctrines
and traditions we've been locked in -
killing offspring with generational trauma.
The genes we share are stained
I was raised a mercenary
a slave to someone else's pain.

MAN

September 23rd 2011

What Would Jesus Do?

What would Jesus do?
Left trembling from the hand of his abuser.
What is his future if all he sees is dealers and users?
He lives in confusion because teachers at school
see the problems but won't offer solutions.

What would Jesus do?
Divorce rates are sky high
but the youth are still being groomed
in a world where only money makes
miracles and dreams come true.
So the yute man are making P's from Q's
it's deets for coupes.
And they're so hungry but still
politicians won't feed them food.
So every time I pray now I'm
trying to find out who I'm speaking to
what would Jesus do?
On a level -

In a world where sex sells
putting your soul for sale is the only way to excel
your people just want to exhale because
we can't breathe.
Can't wear your hearts on sleeves
when your skin is a disease.
Mother's on knees like *Jesus please*
our Fathers
who art in prison
aren't omnipresent to put presents under trees.

Because clear is the correlation
of complexion and convictions
what would Jesus do seeing all of these crucifixions?

What would Jesus do?
If he was born post slavery
born post world wars
born post Internet
where people post daily
deception and their bullshit.
The world goes for seconds of the soup made of fools spit
and pastors telling lies from the pulpit.
When the serpent's tongue is at the end of your thumb
would he still be forgiving and compassionate?
Or would it render him numb?

What if Jesus
was broken into pieces
and the bloodshed received got the treatment it needed?
In the physical he healed but his mind was left feeling
like time had no reason
life had no season.

Walking In The Rain

Being black is
walking in the rain
the rain is heavy
the rain is blood
the blood stains
you have no clothes to change
home is not in range
you're just
walking in the rain.

Feel. Free. Rich.

I woke up feeling fresh
with that new slave mentality
might blow my whole pay cheque
because I slave for my salary.
Poke more holes inside this debt
my only hope is saving sanity
I spend too much on clothes and creps
I'm only aiding my vanity.

That's because all of my real goals
come with two keepers in them.
They designed our socio-economics
and do all they can to keep us in them.
Black capitalism.
Money is our true religion
in our genes it was written
that we would grow to listen
to men with wrists that glisten
then resort to risking prison;
possession with intent
but our only intent was to get
these possessions in an instant.
But it always seems out of reach
why does freedom feel so distant?

I thought this car would make me feel free
this house would make me feel free
thought my tax code
postcode and dress code
would make me feel free.

Thought a watch and chain
and fame would make me feel free
all the knowledge I've attained
I thought my brain would make me feel free.
Praying and paying tithes
this suit and this tie
knife and fork
polite laughing
never ranting
football chanting
my self expression
culture and my art
passport
work rate
slave master's surname
white Jesus
Adam and Eve
Brazilian weave
I thought my degree would make me feel free.

I thought if only they could see me
with badges, motifs and emblems
that resemble those on tv
and concepts tied to western success
that maybe
just maybe they would see me equally.

Black In Babylon

"We refuse to be what you wanted us to be. We are what we are and that's the way it's going to be" – *Bob Marley, 'Babylon System'.*

Whilst preparing for life after university, an old friend asked me are you going to cut off your locs before you graduate? Before I responded, I considered a world of reasons for him asking. That one question at that specific moment in my life confirmed my many thoughts about my friend. But on a deeper level, just the question alone taught me so much about being a black man in this world.

At the time of the question, this old friend of mine was already successful as far as common perception goes; a lifelong A* student with a PhD, now in a career where he rarely comes into contact with other black people. He was clean cut, baby faced and unassuming. His image was monotone, he was afraid. Afraid of raising the volume, afraid of being seen. I lived under a different sky; a law student with no care for pursuing a career in court. I was uncombed, expressive and subversive. I was the look of dynamic and unafraid. Together, we were the image of an odd couple.

We didn't agree on outfit or insight, yet we were friends. The kind of friends that held resistance to one another's ideals. He was a firm believer that there is a uniform and a set route to a black man realising success in the world. The route he chose was one where you don't make noise and you don't challenge. But you do take what is given, you wait for permission and you feel but never speak. He trusted in his path and I trusted his status, suits and shiny shoes were enough for him to valet his blackness on the way into work. I was younger than him, I had observed my friend closely for years. I knew his path was not for me.

My answer to his question was terse, quite simply *no. Man, they're going to think you're difficult, they'll think you smoke Ganja.* He went on to ask if I would go by David, my Christian name. Ty'rone is often mispronounced, the apostrophe stumps people. He told me I would get on better going by David, the simple name. My answer remained the same, no. I was of the mind that my hair and name would be of no relevance in my working life. Of course, I was wrong.

I remember I was one of four key speakers at an event; I walked into the venue and it was filled with suit wearing white people. When I looked at the programme, I noticed it had my name, my job and my degree. I have no idea what the other speakers studied as it only had their name and title. I paid it no mind until that walk from my table to the stage; after being introduced as *poet and law graduate, Ty'rone Haughton.*

Stood on stage, staring at these professional white faces, I realised the moderator had qualified me to the audience. The event and my talk had nothing to do with law, the qualifications of the other speakers were not mentioned and the bio I sent weeks ahead said nothing about a degree. I was there as a poet, to speak about poetry. The others were there to speak about their professions. But, why was it only my presence in need of validation? Would I not be worth listening to had I not graduated?

A black man's success is based on how comfortable he makes white people feel. On how easy he makes things for them. It is based on how well he fits into their limited role of what a black man should be. But it is not freedom if we are told how to be free. I think it's the reason why the country champions Anthony Joshua but I'm not sure they would do the same for Anthony Oluwafemi Olaseni Joshua. The deep love for Mo Farrah may not be extended to Mohamed Muktar Jama Farah. It feels like the less of ourselves we are, the more valuable we are.

This lesson was taught to me upon entry to the UK. No more than a month into my British schooling life, permanently excluded as a four year old. Of course, in typical British fashion, the poison was politely administered. It was under the guise of *we're going to give Ty'rone six months off school – just to give him a chance to lose his accent.*

All my life this country has told me to tuck parts of myself, hide who I am and gentrify my identity. As long as my skin is the only reminder of my blackness, I'd be alright. If I could somehow get used to the *ooh exotic* and the *I don't like spicy food* comments every time I bring Cornmeal porridge to the staff room, I'd be in the good books. If I have a strong threshold for the *does your hair just grow like that?* and *do you mind if I just call you...* conversations, I could go far in this land.

My old friend went far. He believed the ultimate goal of a black man is to assimilate and be accepted by white people. My old friend was desperately wrong. The goal for any black man in Babylon is to freely be himself. To express every trace of his being; to breathe air, cry tears and speak fire. The goal is to love and be loved. To be respected as any other man would. It is not the goal to be palatable and bitesize your blackness.

What he had asked me originally, was not about hair or names.

It was much more than that. I think what he was truly seeking was more like "are you going to proudly showcase your blackness and chase after your dreams without conforming?" Had my old friend asked me that, my answer would have been quite simply, *yes*.

More Fire

Bun Romans and Babylonians
who inflicted colonialism on my black organism.
I can't forgive them
they warped religion and blurred my vision.

Had me stitched into their twisted system.

They taught me
they done more
than any Moor
locked in a morgue.
Then sampled what my people made
and made it something my people can't afford.
In hiding our great inventors
they must be relentless
because that list is so extensive.
A lot of money is made from our intellectual property.

But a black man's soul is so not expensive.

We are just
cheap meat at the market
white punters kick an ugly penny for my carcass.
It's marvellous how
that mindset is a part of us now
we walk as broken kings.

So far from our crowns.

That's why we feel
stuck on potential
nothing named successful.
It's too stressful trying to make it out of this cesspool
aiming to be accepted by white faces in high places
thinking -
my polite graces might erase this
awkward feeling that we both share.
Slave auction, we were both there.
Just had a different reasoning
different colours
different palette
food has a different seasoning.

So, the Caribbean Sea stirs
with the blood of my ancestors
seabed filled with black sons and daughters.

And you wonder why black man *fraid ah wata?*

I am not your negro.
Not your villain.
Not your anti hero.
I am not your prisoner.
Not your cellmate.
Not your cultural food bank.
I am not your menace.
Not your blemish.
I am not your fetish.
Not your entertainment.
Not your athlete.
Nor am I your token.

I was and am still king.

Still got the power of the sun in the pigment of my skin.
my blood
is still Detroit Red
my words
are James Baldwin live in the flesh.
I am every year Nelson Mandela spent in a cell.
I am Darcus Howe
still running the *Race Today*
and my pace is only getting quicker
catching up to the *White Tribe* like -
"Who You Callin' A Nigger?"

I am every single wave
swaying the slaves
from Kunta Kinte Island and Sierra Leone.
I am the fear of the unknown
the power of the sun ignites my soul
I am whole.
Never been three fifths of no man
my mind is expansive
it can never fit into the grips of your hands.

But why must you treat me different?
Is it simply just my pigment?
It's not a figment of my imagination
you'd be ignorant to say
we're not living in a malignant type of nation.

Why must you move the goalposts?
Yet expect me to score most?

We all inhabit the same space
only difference; you inherited a map to this maze.
So we feel like we're still trapped in this cage

because white forefathers believed
there are shades to the ways people behave.

I was born human.
I crawled my way to black.
Now I walk as a nigger.
Everyday I feel blacker
and blacker.
These views all came from you
I came into this world pure hearted.

You cannot undo what you started.

BLAKKA

Black like Noah.
Black man on the ark.
Black like the colour.
Black like noir.

Blacker than *Men In Black*.
tell appropriation to put my melanin back
because I was born permanently dressed in Black.

Black like Tiger Woods
had he known he was Black.
Black as OJ
orange really is the new Black.

Black like diabetes and sickle cell
and chicken and watermelon.
I am Black
like a felon.

Blacker than all the Kardashians cornrows
Black like Michael Jackson had he kept his born nose.
Black as Django.
Black as Shaft.
Catch me in a Black Kangol cap
Black is back.

Son of a gun
I am blacker than a weapon.
Black is a fetish
Black is a blessing

Black is stressing
Black can't hear lesson
Black is fractured
Black is knackered
Black is sick and tired of getting fired at
white cops blacking out on Black children
without a cause.
Who is guilty?
Who is innocent?

You don't even have to be police
you could be a civilian.
He looked suspicious in that hoodie -
the rationale of George Zimmerman.
Please tell me the type of world we're living in
where that kind of killing is acquitted.
Who is guilty?
Who is innocent?

From high yellow.
Dundus.
Black as midnight.
Moonlight makes you blue
I am just as Black as you.
No such thing as light and dark.
Nothing fair about our skin
when the world sees you as sin.
Different shades but we are all
the same Black from within.

Thirteen

Barbershop owners
those with diplomas
spiritual healers
drug dealers
hair weavers.
It's unfair the way they treat us.
Politicians and soldiers
who told us
their country needs you.
But if you make a mistake
on front page
they will say
their country didn't breed you.

Black lives don't matter
they put black lives on a platter
at the Devil's last supper.
There will be a weeping
and a moaning
and a gnashing of teeth.
We often find protection in ourselves
because there's no safety in these streets
from the national police.

'Twas systematic
both sides of the Atlantic
white
blue the
red out of
black.

Your stripes and your stars
scribed the lines of our scars.
And there is no unison in your Union.

Therefore,
I will never fight for your flag or your queen
my flag is black
it's gold
and it's green.

Greed

Every time I eat
it's way more than I need.
It's this greed
more potent than any foreign disease.
I wonder
will I ever be freed
from this western philosophy
which states -
money controls everything
including you and me.

Rae Town

Dreams:

I visit the small place I'm from
will it ever hold me tall like John Lennon?
A Legend?
Adore me as Mandela?
A Robin Hood type figure
someone who came from the bottom.
Someone who left
came back
never forget them.
Someone who made it, if I do
gave back
stayed true
the heart to make it better
but never truly knowing what to do.

Reality:

They can see it in my step
I've clocked how they look at my style.
They can peep the regret
through this crooked smile.
They look at me as a fraud
these streets I was born on now make me paranoid.
I am not Jamaican
enough.
I am a little
too English.

Not enough yard in me
I am a little
too distinguished.
My Accent was relinquished
a little too foreign
a little too bohemian for this part of the Caribbean.

Is my downtown now a little too uptown?
Is my old still a little new?
Will I still dispose of things that could be fitting you?
Is my starvation still satisfied?
Is my poor still getting by?
Is my discomfort still comforting?
Are my nothings still something?
Is my dirty still clean?
My kind still mean?
Is my perspective truly perplexing?
My mirror is losing reflection.

Too Red

As I look for reasons to separate myself
from these perfect possessions
was it worth these expensive lessons?
Jacket too red
jeans too blue
barely ever wore them.
I look at you
jacket, not red enough
jeans, weren't supposed to be stonewashed.
My jaw drops when I hear there used to be denim in them.
The colour was hand washed away
your people being pimped by foreigners exploiting the poor
is just a small price to pay.

My jacket is football red
jeans - electric blue.
I've spoiled myself dead
I accept this truth.
I worked seven days to get this
wore it for four then thought forget this
left it neglected.
You can't trust me to value and cherish this
it's senseless.

I'm not rich but to you I am far from basic
I was picked to be the glitch in the matrix
the car that blitzed off the skalextric.
Only to find refuge in making the excuse that it's
too red, too blue, too old
it's just too new.

Everyone is wearing it
and I'm clearly too good to.
But if we observe the cards I was served
it wouldn't be absurd to say
I deserve to have my jacket too red
I could have ended up dead.
You know what I went through
to have my jeans too blue.

When I hand you this package of two items overpriced
I might hit you with a little lie when you ask why.
I bought them but thought they'd look better on you
or do you want the truth?
Jacket, too red.
Jeans, too blue.

I Don't Look Like Me

I have been frozen   minced and cured
               corned and canned.

              Left to dry, smoke and ferment.

I look like everything I have and have not yet processed.

Perfect Teeth

I never had perfect teeth.
I never lived in a perfect house
on a perfect street
with perfect trees
equipped with perfect leaves.
I was never blessed with perfect teeth.
Gaps in my smile are like voids in my life
something's missing
they all need filling
but I've grown accustomed to this awkward feeling.
Ignoring healing
leaving me enormously revealing.

I chose to never have braces.
Thought I might as well embrace it
plus, you can't hide from life
at times you might have to face it.
Yet no one ever says it
at least not around me.
I feel demons surround me
if I don't look for a while
the goblins gather and natter
about the crooks in my smile.
Though they never express it
they are mighty suggestive
that I should really pull it all together
and get them connected.
Because things are harder to reconnect with
the longer they're neglected.

I never had perfect teeth.
I was never planted with perfect seeds
and blossomed around perfect leaves
truth is, once rooted
I was entangled with imperfect weeds.
A bastard child at first
I almost died at birth
I was never a perfect breed.

Black Boy Blues

For Dea-John Reid

Black boy blues.
They see us hanging and want to make us strange fruit.
What's a black boy to do?
Any time we group
we're called a black boy crew
is it criminal to have a black boy hue?

Black boy blues.
They crop our existence on the evening news
even when we're the victim they make us look accused.
Guilty until proven innocent amongst a jury of sneers
are the black boy rules.

Black boy blues.
I see the game of life is set to make a black boy lose.
Innocent white lies but we get persecuted
for our black boys truths.
No freedom in body or mind
the world turns a blind eye
to my black boy views.

Black boys in any society
are not allowed to play any role other than aggressor.
We are branded as lesser
with double the portion of expectation.
There is nothing like black boy pressure.

Inherited ignorance has been the linchpin
for modern lynchings.

Upheld ignorance is your hindrance to seeing me as full.
Seeing me as rounded.

Will you ever see me as an unabridged man?
Birthed into the same earth the same way you were
or will I remain something you refuse to understand?

Black boy blues.

FATHER

November 29th 2020

New Traditions

What a blessing this boy or girl is
I wonder what your message to the world is.
There's no pressure
I still don't know my purpose.
Destinations aren't important
there's more pleasure in the journeys.

This year I'm turning twenty seven
mum's twenty five
both unlearning all the lessons
for you to live a better life.
Building discernment so we know
which patterns to recognise
unearthing all the happenings
that were once swept aside.

We're old enough to teach
but always young enough to learn.
Your worth on this world
they will tell you is what you earn.
But never chase pennies
do whatever your soul yearns.
May your life be limitless
I don't know how this race of life finishes
but I'll train you to be the faster me.
Run wild and free
young child of glee.
I'm inspired to sing and find you a loving key
because you've ignited the highest of love in me.

I cannot wait for you to see the beauties of life
the stars that swipe through the sky
or the morning sun on the rise.
I want to see your eyes
when you realise clouds move
and cows moo.
And for you to learn the rhythm
of the laughter that surrounds you.
I want to watch you love your mother as much as I do
all the love I have
I will stuff it all inside you.

I was not taught how to play this position
no father figures all the years I've been living.
No inherited precedence, I had to form my own opinions
I can't wait for us to start our own traditions.
My mission switched from making it big
to making it home.
Your story is one of healing and harmony
the greatest love my soul has ever known
onto you we bestow
the goodness from the marrow of our bones.
And in return I'm -
asking you for nothing.
You have no shoes to fill or footsteps to follow
you are not the redemption of my sins
or how to correct tomorrow's.
You are not your parent's past
you get to define yourself
in a world that's so vast
please, go and find yourself.

I pray the resting heartbeat in this Moses basket
will never be in denial
don't sail away from me, my child.
No longer are there lonely magpies in my sights
only joy and light fill my skies
I want you to feel this love that created life.

Daddy Don't Dance

Daddy don't dance
he just pulls up his pants
and -
does the rockaway.
He *leans* back so far you'd forget he's there
anytime it gets musical
he's the first to grab a chair.
And he *stares*
at all their steps
how are they getting them so correct?
Every time they're going right
he's going left.
So he's stressed
it's best
he just sits this one out again.
Watch from a distance
think - what he would do if he were them.

Daddy wants to dance like the Cubans
all the passion I possess
I want to put it into movement.
I want to turn my tense frame into something fluid
to put my emotions into motion
rolling from my shoulders
embolden my hips to flow with the whine I'm holding.

Daddy wants to dance like Freddie Mercury
performing *'Don't Stop Me Now'.*
Or James Brown - wowing the crowd
he's tryna' *get up offa that thing*

he knows dance will make him feel better.
But better yet he's still stuck to the seat
nods to the beat
silent taps of the feet.

Daddy wants to take your mother out dancing
in loose fitted clothing
I want to keep going
until the music stops and the bar starts closing.
Will she ever see me lose all inhibitions?
Move how I envision?
The cruellest disposition is to learn you've not been living
in this body you've been given.

You're smitten with music
I'm sitting as usual
watching you groove to new soundscapes
I wear my proud face
as you mount your mum's waist.
Both swaying
twirling and playing.
You send me inviting looks
showing me the way in.
Each time I knock down a glance
the more you learn
daddy don't dance.

At a young age
daddy got dashed off stage
for having no rhythm
of course that caused that ism.
To make my body feel like prison.
Flesh and mind are not in alignment
daddy don't dance because he's trapped in his own confinement.

HOODS

May all your hoods be beautiful.
I hope they suit you well
a perfect fit for all hoods you're in
here's to hoping the fabric manoeuvres
into the grooves of your skin.
Your hoods
will cover you with the teachings of your past
the seedlings planted
will grow trees with leaves and branches
laden with fruit to feed your hoods.

I hope your hoods protect you
from any rain that may surely come.
Remember
any hood you're wearing
or any hood you're from
brings prejudice, stereotypes
not for you to prove wrong.
Just prove yourself right.
But don't be self righteous
because these hoods have a way
of coming back to bite us.

These hoods make us
everything we are.
Hoods shape and dictate
the messages of our heart
the thoughts in our minds
and our inward voices.

These hoods
have already made our choices.
Already set our challenges
our life chances balances on
what we dance with in our hoods.
Our future is just fruition of the bads and the goods
of our pasts'.

Please understand
whether you are child, father or man
these hoods share strands
each action is pre-planned.
They are tied to one another
there is a suture sewn to suit you
our parent's past becomes our future
we are tasked to see you lose
the bruises of our youth.
Clearing the way for you to find your truth.

Pain & Privilege

All of our losses were just lectures and lessons
regardless of what it cost us
we must accept this as a blessing.
We are both from broken homes; cracked foundations.
Together, we made one whole that still needed renovations.
All we are is fractions
fractured by childhoods filled with bad reactions
poor attachments
incidents of abuse
which stole the innocence of our youth.

In a sense, we put our wounds to good use
refused to let our pain be reused
by him and by you.
What we had was pain
what you have is privilege.
Parents who made a lot from their little bits
made middle class little kids
not with silver spoon but with wriggle room
to grow and be you.
And the space to make mistakes
knowing you will always be assuredly safe.

Two fractured fractions -
she is three fourths
I am barely a quarter.
Both from broken homes
too damaged alone to ever get sold
but we put our fragments together
and we made one whole.

In The Middle

Somewhere
in the middle of the country
in the middle of the street
just off the main road.

There is a house where,
in the middle of the night
cries a newborn
hungry for mother's milk.
The crack pipe pops out in front of a mother's offspring.
Midwives love the jazz - the plants and art.
Police try to bring calm to disputes
families always fight at Christmas
but this year we're here to celebrate the brightest gift.

There is a house where,
in the middle of the night
tired eyed parents find new ways to love.
Old patterns and cycles still evoke pain.
There is water and thirst
food and hunger
mother and baby
learning the latch.
Ambulance sirens sneak quietly through the blinds
a sobering end to the night
but let us hold onto to this high
there's no notice for when it's the last time.

There is a house where,
in the middle of the day

sunlight storifies the night that just left.
Eyes black and eyes red
we're all blinded by love.
The days show our view is the same
but in perspective
there's change.
There's parallel lanes
a set of destinies going separate ways.
There's the worst and best
cursed and blessed
birth and death
dance in unison step
under the glance of the same moon.

This all happens somewhere
in the middle of the country
in the middle of the street just off the main road
there's a wall in the middle of two terraced territories.
Twins, if you will
the interior is where the difference is.
We share many similarities
yet have many more differences.

The Village

"A village has to raise these young kings and queens to believe their greatness." - Kano, 'Teardrops'.

As the days were drawing closer to my son being born. I could not stop thinking about what life was going to be like for him. I would spend most of my days playing through scenarios that he will never experience. Would his childhood be like my own? No, how could I ever let that be? Would he ever feel abandoned? No, but there would be a sense of displacement that I would feel for him.

Looking back to when I was sent to England; I know that decision changed my life forever, in ways I am sure nobody expected. At four years old, loss and mourning became permanent fixtures in my future life. Nobody knew I would be deprived of so much time with my family, or how separation has a direct impact on how we relate to one another. I felt the loss of experience and my son will feel the loss of opportunity. The opportunity to eat his grandmother's Rum Cake, his aunt's Hominy Corn Porridge or his great grandmother's *anything!* He may never know the loss because he has never tasted it. He will never live in the village.

The village that raises children and teaches them how to operate in this world. Our babies are our own but they belong to the villages we put them in. They support parents financially, physically and emotionally. They help feed, protect and teach our children. We need the village and the village needs our children to continue raising good citizens of the world.

My son only knows his mother's family as his village, they buy him gifts, spend time with him, Christmases and all other occasions. It makes me feel the need to overcompensate. I feel as though I need to be his father but also all the village folk he has no contact with. I alone must contribute as much as his mother's family does in order for me to not feel his loss. I heard no man is an island, but can a man be a village? I comfort myself thinking the answer is yes. I feel I am a better cook than my mother and Aunt so that evens out the loss of a Rum Cake and some porridge. My granny though... that is a loss we will both share.

I am aware of the distinction I make between my son's mother's village and my own. I know we share a village but I cannot shake the question – if I have no accessible family, who will be my son's village? It's not so much about who but more so who do I trust to care for my child in the way I do. The biggest realisation for me was that the questions and scenarios I pondered leading up to his birth, were actually not about him – it was all me.

The village I was raised in was rotten, corrupt and evil. It was an actual family but the antithesis of what you think when you hear 'family'. They were but should not have been trusted to care for me, teach me or protect me. Clearly my views on family are skewed. I honestly do not feel anything for most of my relatives, it's like a void that I physically feel, almost as if we can't relate on anything. My whole life I have observed my family and others as an outsider and I hate them all. I hate the dutifulness, the acceptance, the active ignorance, the "just cause" and shoulder shrugging that comes with families.

But now, I am faced with my own family, whom I love. My son's mother brings with her a matriarchy, a village of fiercely loving women who love him in the way big cats love their cubs. I bring a shameful, abusive and neglectful family. He doesn't need my village. He needs me to dive into his mother's waters and learn her customs. He needs me to join the village feast and bring my own pot to share with all. I need me to join.

Thank You

For your touches.
Strokes, leg rests and secret squeezes
I didn't know I needed.
They each sing a song of safety to my body
with words I'm still learning.
For your love.
One I thought could never be mine
a source of unconditional affection.
I thank you.
For your understanding.
I don't have to tell for you to know
it happened quick -
you took a print of my mind
like hands pressed in snow.
For your time.
Spent and shared
given and taken
to fancy my light
but to know my dark
I thank you.
For your mothering.
Watching you nurture is healing
the sore boy I hold within me.
For your patience.
Gracefully waiting for me to believe you are real
I thank you.

Bonsai

Black man seed plant Bonsai tree
that must be
the only one I see.
Show me one forest
Bonsai can flourish.
Biggest fear
plant Bonsai
I cannot nourish.
Though, I shan't worry or be discouraged
planting seeds is such a luxury.

White man seed plant tree like Oak
they make forests which are filled with hope.
They reach heights just nigh of heaven
I may never see the things they have forgotten.
Oak tree roots spread the breadth of the earth
whilst I must attest
I was blessed with this curse.
Though, I shan't worry or be discouraged
planting seeds is such a luxury.

White man forest can take over land
while my Bonsai roots lay in the palm of his hand.
Bonsai grow strong
seldom grow long.
Even when held with an outstretched arm
misguiding is vertigo
we still have so far to go.
Bonsai only grow
as high as they'll allow

when they have taken all you have to offer
they will drop you
you will fall.
In all your gorgeous encased glory.
You -
have now met the end of your story.
But you made tiny roots and branches
you didn't want to leave them stranded.
Will this be what concludes your legacy?

Though, you shan't worry or be discouraged
planting seeds is such a luxury.
But planting seeds is not enough for me
because my seed might receive gunshot flurry
from cowards with man made powers.
They could stop my seed growing to a beautiful flower.
I rose from concrete and barbed wire
one Bonsai trying to grow a little higher
but sirens and badges
could catch my seed in traffic
couple rounds could see his blood splattered.

Or knee to the neck until *I can't breathe.*

It's so tragic
this happens all over the planet
Bonsai held to a totally different standard.

Volvo

Do all fathers drive Volvos?
It looks like it
preoccupied dads trying to stay present behind the wheel.
Quick glance at the empty car seat in back
a constant reminder of what's real
a reminder of why style was sacrificed for stability.
Life has meaning when you smile
and I see a little me
growing in a world so cold
I need to hold my family close.

Are all fathers just guns on safety?
Used to bang if you threaten
nowadays he's more symbol than weapon
can't be alarmed and can't be triggered
please remain calm
the wrong decision may harm these children.
Might scar their existence
one bad move could tarnish their experience.
Do all fathers' instincts become inconvenience?

Do all fathers have to be the bigger man?
Ignore our kneejerk
assess our thoughts and re-word?
I have never backed down
I have never walked
I run to the fight
I'm too proud to let it slide
but this home cannot house pride.
Do all fathers try to be angels
and leave their demons outside?

Are all fathers carrying this pressure?
A lead suit made to measure
we wear it with pleasure.
Though, it handicaps our movements
and shatters our illusions of being superhuman.
Fatherhood: a trying lesson in truth.
I have nothing to prove
I just want to make it home to you.

Spring's Dawn

A Spring's dawn
before the sun is born.
When the landscape paints your face shades of blue and silver
the trees yet to be in bloom are just silhouettes of veins,
lightning, cracks - freedom.
You ask for the moon
and I go find it.

Reach

My son and I play a game called 'REACH'.
I say REACH, with outstretched arms he waits for me to pick
him up - simple enough.

REACH He reaches, I pick him up and take him wherever he
wants to go.
I have always picked him up.

But
the day will come when death and I shall meet
bringing my show to a close and an end to my speech.
But still REACH.

REACH past the stars of the world that I give you.
REACH beyond my shortcomings.
REACH past limitations you may place upon yourself.
REACH over society's expectations.
REACH deep down inside yourself if you ever forget who
you are.

If anything at anytime feels too far
remember the days we would play
REACH!

Footnotes For My Son

The truth is born in the dim light of evenings
neatly weaved into mouthfuls and gulps.
Never around nibbles and sips
inhibition hinders visits from the truth.
It does not mingle with the prim,
the proper and the perfect.
it whispers in the whiskers of the old broom
it is the song of the sufferer.

The truth is rarely told by men.
Especially those with power and privilege
never vouch for them.
But believe in the creak of wood
in the draft under doors
the wrath of water
and the glow of fire.
Trust in summer's sweat
shivers of Winters
and the sound of leaves around your birthday.

The truth is found in forgotten books
in the folds of skin we study on early mornings
stood naked in front of the mirror.
Truth needs no filter or vanity
classroom or corner office
status nor symbol
do not believe in these things, baby boy.

Store trust in your mother's embrace
it will rescue you before you know you are lost.
Trust in your father's word
curated by lifetimes of experience.
Bury your trust deep in the dirt of earth
let the soil fill your fingerprints
allow the elements to do their work.
Only feed on that which is true
it will soon become you.
Always trust in the sun and the moon
they are only more consistent than your mother.

P.S. connect with a higher power, we are nothing without faith.

ACKNOWLEDGEMENTS

Mr Martin, you were right - I eventually found my path. Somehow, you knew I couldn't find the directions to my journey at school. Thank you for believing in me, Sir.

Jay Zorenti-Nakhid - my Pisces Moon brother. I know you refute this but you are the reason this book is published. Your contribution, however you downplay it, has led me to where I am today. I appreciate it and I appreciate you.

My dear Uncle. I want to thank you for being a needed presence in my life. Although, I have and will forever continue to disagree with everything you say; I have learned more from our barbershops debates than any class or lecture.

Bounce, I started writing these poems for you when you were just a foetus; I helped conceive you and in turn, you conceived this book. I thought it would be cool for you to one day have them and find some guidance from your old man - I hope you do. Thank you for the daily inspiration and the nightly writing sessions you facilitated. Some of my greatest work was made whilst putting you back to sleep.

Fin, my wife, my partner in everything. My gratitude cannot fit into a Thank you. You made this possible - from making sure I'm writing to being a soundboard, consultant and one woman audience. My sun doesn't rise without you.

And to you, for reading - thank you. Eternally grateful.

T.

ABOUT VERVE POETRY PRESS

Verve Poetry Press is an award-winning press that focused initially on meeting a local need in Birmingham - a need for the vibrant poetry scene here in Brum to find a way to present itself to the poetry world via publication. Co-founded by Stuart Bartholomew and Amerah Saleh, it now publishes poets from all corners of the UK and beyond - poets that speak to the city's varied and energetic qualities and will contribute to its many poetic stories.

As well as publishing full poetry collections, we have a colourful pamphlet series, many featuring poets who have performed at our sister festival - and a poetry show series which captures the magic of longer poetry performance pieces by festival alumni such as Polarbear, Matt Abbott and Imogen Stirling.

The press has been voted Most Innovative Publisher at the Saboteur Awards, and has won the Publisher's Award for Poetry Pamphlets at the Michael Marks Awards.

Like the festival, we strive to think about poetry in inclusive ways and embrace the multiplicity of approaches towards this glorious art.

www.vervepoetrypress.com
@VervePoetryPres
mail@vervepoetrypress.com